I0417404

Autumn Loves

Written By Diahann Darwood   Illustrated by Niaren Binford

For Autumn, who has arrived with the force of life
For Noah, who loves nature
For Derrell, who inspires
And For Max, who encourages

Copyright © 2016 by Diahann Darwood

All rights reserved. No part of this publication may be reproduced, distributed, or transmitted in any form or by any means, including photocopying, recording, or other electronic or mechanical methods, without the prior written permission of the publisher, except in the case of brief quotations embodied in critical reviews and certain other noncommercial uses permitted by copyright law. For permission requests, write to the publisher, addressed "Attention: Permissions Coordinator," at the address below.

Creation Stirred Inc.
15 Landau Lane
New Hempstead, NY 10977

Printed in the United States of America

First Printing, 2016

ISBN -10: 1-5395-3581-9

ISBN 13: 978-1-5395-3581-2

Autumn, the year's last, loveliest smile.
William Cullen Bryant

American romantic poet, journalist, and editor of the New York Evening Post
1794 - 1878

Do you know what colors Autumn loves to show? Autumn loves red, green, brown, and gold! I know because when I look out my window, I see those colors blow!

Do you know why Autumn blows the leaves around? She loves to put Mr. Tree's leaves on the ground.

So we can run, swish, and jump into a huge, leafy mound!

Do you know what Autumn does to the cool air for everyone?

Autumn loves to mix the chilly air with the bright, bright sun.

Outside is not as warm as the summer, but we can still have fun!

Hmm, I wonder if Autumn has fur like a cat. Because she loves when we wear our sweaters and warm hats.
We can face her brisk wind, and she loves that!

I wonder if Autumn knows winter is next.
Autumn loves to say 'Good-bye' to mosquitoes and insects.
And we say 'Hello' to colorful trees, 'Hello' to fall's best.

Does Autumn think orange is a good luck charm? She loves when we take trips to the nearby farm. That's where she grows the pumpkins I pick and carry in my arms.

I wonder if she is setting a stage for us.
Because Autumn loves that it's time for squirrels to gather nuts.
And we watch them work as we ride back to school on our yellow bus.

I love Autumn and she loves me, I know. We snuggle and drink warm cider while she's all aglow.

Enjoy the season!

Science is Everywhere!

Find out more...

Go on a nature walk. Collect some leaves. What do you see?

Why do most leaves change color in the fall?

What animals hibernate?

Can you...

Create a diorama or illustration of an animal in it's environment?

Visit a farm for apple or pumpkin picking?

Track the weather for 7 days (or more)?

www.ingramcontent.com/pod-product-compliance
Lightning Source LLC
Chambersburg PA
CBHW060817290526

45792CB00005BB/1688